Notes from the Shadow Self

by

Carolyn Wolfe

Cover photo by S. Douglas Wolfe

Avid Readers Publishing Group
Lakewood, California

Notes from the Shadow Self

Avid Readers Publishing Group

http://www.avidreaderspg.com

ISBN-13: 978-1-935105-48-0

Printed in the United States

Acknowledgements

I would like to acknowledge that some of these poems were published in wonderful "Little" and Literary Magazines. These magazines, some of which are now defunct, gave me the courage to publish on my own.

"Little" and Literary Magazines and Newspapers

Orphic Lute
Prophetic Voices
Mind Candy
The City Paper
Legend Magazine (England)

Ezines on the Web

The Web Poets Corner
The Green Silk Journal

Table of Contents

Lady In Sepia

She lives on
Canvas
red hair
dark eyes
beautiful face
not smiling
though
solemn
almost a
pout
her cap
is soft, soft cream
covering her runaway curls
as if remonstrating them
for their errant behavior
A satin ribbon flows down from the side of her cap
down to her shoulder
like a melting icicle
ice against the fire of her hair
whoever saw this portrait
now colored with age
would wonder at her loveliness
and question her solemn demeanor
me,

I just watch her
watching me
with
her cold sepia expression
suddenly unable to defend myself
I leave
almost
hearing
her soft sigh of disapproval...

Dark Tequila Nights

Straight, no ice
in the liquid darkness
no tequila sunrises for me, thank you
I like it late night
stars just out of reach
blurred, twinkling
and the air is thick with Summer's
labored
heat
it is a sweaty affair
no frills
just the tequila and I
enjoying the long, slow ride
of going downhill
each sip
a
raw taste
bringing on
the
overwhelming feeling of
pleasure,
in the darkness.
then slowly,
I slip into a vision
of what I might have
become

had I chosen to
live

in daylight...

Books and Lovers

The book was sipped at
and put down
she crossed her arms in front of her
and savored
the beauty of the words
the dialogue that charmed
like someone she had once known.

some books were meant to be gulped
some chewed over
but this one,
this one,
was meant to be sipped
and savored

this one was meant to last…

unlike someone she had
once known.

White Noise

The sun came loudly into my room today
breaking into my hangover
with an over bright medley of white light
and heat
crashing into my walls
making my curtains misbehave
and trade the cool darkness
for patterns of brilliance
slashing across my windows
so intense was the noise
that my pillow could not restrain it
so I got off my sofa
and limped slowly into the back
room
where some loving and
understanding architect
made sure
there were no windows

to let in
such an unwelcome intruder

as light.

The Picture

The morning is fresh and idealized in my mind
I stop, get out of the car, camera at the ready
looking with it's fresh eye, for an image to present
itself
there it is
a long sleek, metal truck, it's engine off
tiny windows all along it's side
window slat window
the pattern captures my attention
such a redundant, yet perfect pattern
I go closer, lens ready to click
and then eyes, 20 to 50 pair staring straight at me
holding in sadness so remote, it freezes ice
I step back, really looking this time
out pops a head
straining, straining but unable
to escape
this monstrous truck

lambs
it's a hideous transport
a jail
of agonized animals
looking out at the world
who never looks at them

except as chops
perfectly wrapped
to feed unabated appetite
closing my eyes

I took the picture

it was the least I could do

I don't take pictures anymore

The Flower

I picked an October flower
orange and sudden
with remembered life
I turned it into a headdress
so that its' memory
would become
mine.
Thinking only of how lovely
flower knowledge would be…
The last memory
was of sun
of wind
of dew caressing it's petals
then
of a selfish fleshy hand
ripping it asunder

even flowers

cry.

Corners

I see her standing
in the corners of your eyes
this one
this newly met
this sequel.

She stands there

as you reach for me
almost in desperation
as if you seek to embrace
a life jacket
that is drifting
just out of reach…

I see her standing
in the corner
filled with smug assault

You strain for conversation
as if you would practice me
like a piano
out of tune
forgetting lessons
so earnestly learned
by both of us, long ago.

Today
I began to vacuum
at first boldly
then
so afraid
so terribly, honestly afraid
to vacuum

the corners...

SOMETIMES SECOND IS BEST

I am attracted to him

much like a placated color

duller in his presence perhaps,
and milder

I cannot shine
as intensely

but

that is the beauty
of our relationship

for

in relation to him

I am but a blonde star

to his wildly burning

sun.

<u>**HANDS**</u>

At night

my hands become claw-like creatures

that walk crab-like through the sheets

over

to your side of the bed
where they touch your hand
and become soft
and pliable.
Upon residing in the shell-like comfort
of your palm
they slowly return to normal
and
I
sleep.

FUGITIVE HEARTS

The pages of new work

lie unguarded
in the waste basket
the metal rim catches
torn bits of paper
that look like tiny white hands
thrusting through prison bars.

Pages
containing intimate passages
that tell too much
of my real self
too well
are thrown there
to keep the real truth
hidden

even from me

But

when the fan blows
the pages flutter
creating whispers
that sound like voices
of
tiny,
fugitive
hearts.

SUMMER'S HOUSE

This house was built
to shelter shadows
they reach across the room
like tattered clothing
edges
dangling
creating minutes
that stretch for hours
across a noon rug.

Suddenly,
the swift Sundance of evening
overtakes
a lazy afternoon…

I stand up

feeling weak limbed
as I watch my house greet
it's more intimate guests.

I have become a creature
of too much density
and structure
and can only
stand
almost hidden
as the curtain rustles softly.

straining moonlight
through

ribboned hands.

What Cats Dream About

Little kitty
My grocery bag warrior
My winner of little battles
The one who becomes
The soliloquy
Of aggravation
When dinner is a wee bit late…

Master kitty
Little battler of evolution
Tiny dancer
With big cat feet
Come up
Ever so slowly
Because you can't appear
too
Anxious
And sit on my lap
While you dream
What wild cats dream
And stalk the deep green jungles
Of
Instinct…

MATING SEASON

The desperate flirtation
of a Summer's evening

when the air around you
has it's own courting structure
and all structures are meant
to bend

according to each scripture
of self-worth or self-denial.

And all illusions burst forth
much like blossoms breaking the bough
because of their very fullness...

The music you hear
is strained to an almost perfect,
yet unbearably hushed
pitch.

So you dance
to the more intimate steps
of the Summer heat.
You
then
become involved
in the frenzy of discord
and discovery.
that is when the night takes away
all names

and absorbs
you

as its very

own...

EXIT AUTUMN

In the woods
I saw a lady
made of leaves.

Soft brown earth became her hair
highlighted by shimmering red maple.
Her eyes
though half closed
were bright with wisdom.

Silently
she sat there
wrapped in a cocoon of age
and the dreaming sentience
of a softer
change of Season.

As I was leaving the woods
wondering at such a vision
I saw her rustle
very slowly,
and turn

gently giving to me

her powdered
smile.

<u>ASSASSINS OF DESTINY</u>

Sheets pull the wind into them
as they dry in the stagnant heat of midsummer
on the television
a newscaster proclaims
EARTH DAY
was a success.

But
oil runs down the driveway
where the business man parks a junker
likes to work on cars
when he is not office bound.

blue suds bubble in the basement drain
laundry has to be done
plastic diapers reek in the disposal
awaiting garbage day.

Bottles and cans too,
lie amidst the garbage
lucky there's no law yet,

Recycling is such a nuisance anyway…

Janie's fifteen and pregnant
put away her dolls for the real thing
her body is a factory
manufacturing need.

EARTH DAY
was a success,
as far as it goes
But,
ignorance,
laziness,
and
apathy
Rule

sharp as knives
in the hands of a billion
assassins...

MAKE WAR NOT LOVE

My husband,
So in the middle
of the rain of bullets
and stench of blood
you come to me for
love and comfort
these I give freely
I wipe the sweat from your face
even though I cannot
wipe the fear from your eyes...
My husband,
I watch you dance
a silent rhythm
in boots thick with vermin
in clothes red from blood
like no satin sheet can gleam...
I will give you
the warmth of my embrace
the food from my humble kitchen
and my soul

but
Oh, my husband
take only the love offered
in spirit
for I do not offer my body
No lamb from my womb
shall be sacrificed
for a new army of death
No body of mine
shall rear a killer
or a victim
My body was meant to bear a gift
to the stars
but the stars shall not have
their due
Nor shall the hungry beast of war
suckle my babe
with hate for food
and blood as its mother's milk

No babe of mine
shall you beget

Better by far
that I suffer with you
in an unkind world
with no one to carry on
your name
or my eyes
than to become a murderer
disguised as your
lover

WISEWOMAN

She stood alone
half in sun
half
in shadow
a tiny monument of a woman
torn like a bright, white strip
of paper
neatly in two
And so she was a beggar
who had never learned what it was to
beg
until now

And she was a leader
of tiny bright consciousness
illuminating souls
with the vision of
elder past times
Living in a decaying era
she taught the hunt
of the heart
to the few left
who had the strength
and the grace

To stand all at once
in sun
and
shadow

NOT OF THIS TIME

I look at the sunset and say
this is not the time for such brave color
not a time for all those Myths
that glorified each season
and made a conquest of each dawn
my eyes fill with tears
as my heart fills with a longing
unable to be quenched
by the derisive seconds
contained in the mundane reality
that I live daily by
This is not a time for star gazers
yet there are memories
lying fallow
just beneath the surface
begging a listen to
by any receptive ear
I watch the clouds
seeing pictures of forgotten history
and slowly absorb patience
sitting by the great Bay waters
as they rise to greet the beach
the hungry waves assuaged and welcomed
at the same moment
and know a memory

in which we sought a forest of determined survivors
where we spoke the language of common lore
where we had heroes and heroines that spoke more
of
ourselves
than any reflective mirror
and So in my dreams
I reach for Avalon
ride by Robin's side in wooded splendor
an arrow and an eye cocked for danger
and find a universe of old
resting nicely
on the shoulders of my King…

THE MESSAGES OF TREES

Trees are natural transmitters
blowing each stray thought through their leaves
each night waiting softly
waiting silently
for starry answers...

THE ADEPT

Author of the suggestive arts
I see in your hands a crystal
you dangle it carelessly
from your fingers
and as it sways
it sparkles
begins to glow
not of itself
but of the purity
of your power.

TRESPASS

I find I need the fuel of company
to feed me through times of creative famine
and so I build landmarks to trespassers
knowing, as they know
that trespassing is an ancient rite
the pacifier to loneliness
the prelude to sharing
as each jarring note of injured privacy
becomes a beginning place
for the footsteps of the spirit
entering in a new phase
of uncharted emotions
And so Trespass is a sacred word
reminding me of
warmth, nurturing and renewal.

Fantasies Involving an Unknown Party Guest

Having seen the artistry of your
Smile
I confess to a certain weakness
Though a woman's weakness is not any
News to you
I am sure

I have to hand it to you
Your eyes have all the light in the room
At their disposal
I see you have the good grace
To blush
Almost modestly
And yet somehow
I expect
You are not quite
As bashful as you seem
But that
Could be only wishful thinking
On my part
And somehow
I believe that all the dreams
I have tonight
Will be featuring you
In a
Prominent
position

<u>**Newcomers**</u>

Winter walks in with the new customers
A chill is left
In the newcomers jacket
Giving a brisk squeeze
To the warmth of the room
Smiles freeze
For just a moment
Until the stranger passes

His jacket is tossed
On the back of his chair
his mouth
closing in
on liquid warmth
Sweeter than a kiss
In this moment at least

Only then does he look
for that second best sweet
Another drink
And the warmth fills that need
Another
And the quest for a kiss
Is forgotten
Folded and pocketed
Until he feels
The cold wind
Blowing in
On the jacket
Of an attractive

Newcomer.

Tis The Season

In the Winter
The city shivers
Like a
Woman with no lover,
A man with no child to come home to
Like a bereft dancer
Who has lost her step
mid-dance
Center stage

Christmas
Causes the branches of the city
To wear braces
Of tinsel teeth
Which look almost ugly
Trying to keep
The spirit alive
Snow turns to grit
Grit
turns into a dangerous ice phase
And the squeal of tires
Becomes
As common
As Christmas carols on a
Noonday street

And in the place
Where no one is looking
There is no Christmas
Only sadness, despair and longing
Looking at the glitz and glamour
With eyes dull
From pain

Christmas in the city
Gives lonliness
A bad name…

Broken Lanterns

Sometimes
He stands in the rain
Trying to pocket the light
A street lamp offers
So he can fill himself up again
And get that glow on

At night
His thoughts circle
Lonely backyard alleyways
In search of broken lanterns
That he could fix

But in his heart
He hopes
To find only shattered glass
Having lost his ability
To put things right
Long ago.

Withered Leaves

The withered leaves
Press against the glass
Fervent with anguish
And hell bent on getting inside

The leaves
Like an old man's palm
Wrenched at the window
Battering against it
Uselessly
Yet creating an atmosphere
Of barely contained violence

And somehow
One knew
They would eventually
Get inside.

A Nostalgic Viewpoint

I believe
it is almost an unconscious thing
this unpardonable nostalgia
this sadness for days gone by
One looks at the land
and feels the loss of discarded souls there
giving the land a misbegotten essence to it
as if it is leftover
and not new
no longer eternal
it is only a potential victim
slated for slaughter
I guess our sadness must come from the fact
that it is our hands
that commit this murder
the land cries for renewal
but we cry
for what we can no longer pity...

For The Love of Dolphins

Somebody once said
That my symbol was the dolphin
And I was in love with that thought
Glad to have a connection
With those beautiful
Trusting, creatures
Not entirely bound by water
nor air
Sleek, intelligent
Wise beyond the tender years of man

Being city bred
I could only watch my aqua-other
On TV
In black and white
And later
In living color
At Sea-World

But every Summer
When I came to the beach
I would look for them
In vain

Until this year
I finally viewed
The graceful arch of traveling porpoise
Many and many in a day they came
And I thought myself
Truly blessed
Until…
I heard on the evening news
Pollution had taken it's toll
Dolphins lying still
On lonely sands

No longer creatures of water

Or air

Discontent

We live in the shadow
Of each other's
Discontent
But the pattern of your blue panic
Undoes me
In it's simplicity
Self destruction is such an anti-climax
Hiding truths
So well spoken
They sound like a lie

Gazing into one another
Seeing pasts that belong only
In the singular
Each blaming each
For all the lost years
Discontent and restless
We are still reaching for stars
That have long ago died

But what is left
Is only
Illusional star power
Crossing universal miles

The stars themselves
Having long ago moved on
To a higher destination
Higher than sky
Higher than moon
Higher than hopes

And we
Landbound
Can only
Watch and dream
About

Leftover starlight…

Aftermath

The division
Of a dream combined
Creates
A chasm
For indifference
To slowly grow

Bright images fade
Passions ignite
Leaving behind a vast wateland
Desolate of anything
But dust

Where there was life
There is dust
Where there was love
There is dust
It center its orbit
In the blankness of your eyes
And corrupts
The sweetness of your smile

A void
A dead sar
A black hole
The aftermath of romance
Is written in
Our galaxy's
Design…

Gallery

She sips chamomile
And breathes out
Flowered breath
As she reels her hours
In impressionistic splendor

Her dress of lace
Falls
To the right ankle length
As she peruses the museum
Walking slowly
As if in a garden
That is
Flowering
Ripening
Falling
Blossoming too full

Just like herself
As she steps
Out of the doorway
Down the steps
Into the
Oily city streets
Back into reality
Still kicking fallen blossoms
From her shoes…

Making Change

Talking to the cashier
she said
Things have got to change soon
I am beginning to feel like the leech- woman
hanging on to bad relationships
which keep dumping salt on me
"Quick get her off"
they say
but me
despite the seasoning, I hang on
And let me tell you
the old bad habits
are getting boring
I'm searching for new mistakes
sort of a reverse birthing process
and looking to get further behind
'cause looking ahead
is way too taxing
and ha ha, I haven't paid taxes in years
I could lead a life of quiet desperation
or not so quiet belligerence
but who would notice the difference?
Instead I
cash and carry
and off load my woes
on all who come near
my wading pool of self pity
what?

Oh I digress
can I have change for a dollar?
as she leaves
she never notices the people in line
that had been behind her
hiss and crackle like cellophane
and the cashier hands her a blank check of a stare
but she just walks away,
and feels relieved,
as she makes her way down the street,

jingling her change...

Imprisoned

Up here
My cat looks outside
From an inside
Window ledge
Staring down
At the courtyard
Where a million shrieking birds
Swoop and holler

Enraged
My cat does a slow window dance
Tail twitching, eyes slit
Claws coiled
As each taunting caw
Moves visibly across his back
Like a bristling wave
Of anxiety

As the birds flutter
Coy insults
At their impotent
Enemy
His tail slithers down

And the gold-green eyes
Turn
And gaze at their jailor
In calculating fury

I leave the room quickly
Still gasping at my new title…

The Larger Thing

Lunch, down by the waterfront
where the water has taken on the color of light
The grey of the sky clouds
and the white of the tumbled rocks
that barrier the water
from the park

It is a gentle place
people are having lunch from a picnic basket,
walking, running, sharing special moments
but the conversation,
when there is any
is hushed
This is a place of peace

As I look deeper into the water
I see other shades within it
I see the grey of mist
of concrete
of steel
It appears to melt all the city's disappointments
into itself
and then release it
So that we
who look deeply into it's waters
gather strength
from it's reflection

Out at the far edge of the water
a bright red tour boat
rolls by
a distant hum
on the grey calm
It's vibrant colors
tease their reflection
along the waves
as if to share
the joy of red
with the ashen colored water

There is a shared purpose here
Industry quiets
loses itself
in the contemplation of larger issues
other than the legal tender

and I realize
What fate brought me here
to this loveliness
will deliver me
to a greater tomorrow

But for now

I sit here
and journey away from my workplace
feeling a sense of continuity
with nature
with a thing that is beyond myself
beyond the ebb and flow
of a 9-5 existence

and so I sit here
a casual admirer
of the larger thing...

A Question of Time

The bar
Stutters behind me
Swilling warm beer
Swallowing cold pizza
I glance at my watch
And wait for you

The evening catches on
People slide past
Pretty girls ripe for lovers
Older married women
Wishing they were pretty girls
And I glance at my watch
Wishing you were here

The evening bends into
A long, lethargic creep
My pitcher of beer diminishing
I wonder where you are

It is now the edge of morning
Candles sputter and threaten
To blow out
Smiling men usher
Lonely women through the doorway
Until
Only I am left here
Watch dangling
Cursing the numerals
That broke the evening's back…

www.ingramcontent.com/pod-product-compliance
Lightning Source LLC
LaVergne TN
LVHW050944080826
845145LV00004B/1407
9781935105480